THE
TITANIC

Sarah Blackmore

Published in association with The Basic Skills Agency

Hodder & Stoughton
A MEMBER OF THE HODDER HEADLINE GROUP

Acknowledgements

Cover: Photodisc

Photos: pp 2, 28 Mary Evans Picture Library; pp 5, 24 Hulton Getty; pp 7, 9, 13, 27 Popperfoto

Every effort has been made to trace copyright holders of material reproduced in this book. Any rights not acknowledged will be acknowledged in subsequent printings if notice is given to the publisher.

Orders; please contact Bookpoint Ltd, 130 Milton Park, Abingdon, Oxon OX14 4SB. Telephone: (44) 01235 400414, Fax: (44) 01235 400454. Lines are open from 9.00–6.00, Monday to Saturday, with a 24 hour message answering service. You can also order through our website: www.hodderheadline.co.uk

British Library Cataloguing in Publication Data
A catalogue record for this title is available from the British Library

ISBN 0 340 87695 6

First published 2000
This edition published 2003
Impression number   10 9 8 7 6 5 4 3 2 1
Year   2007 2006 2005 2004 2003

Copyright © 1999 NTC/Contemporary Publishing Group, Inc.

Adapted for the Livewire series by Sarah Blackmore

Typeset by SX Composing DTP, Rayleigh, Essex.
Printed in Great Britain for Hodder and Stoughton Educational, a division of Hodder Headline, 338 Euston Road, London NW1 3BH, by The Bath Press, Bath.

Contents

1 The *Titanic*

The *Titanic*.
It was big.
It was really big.
It was a sea-going hotel.
It was the largest ship ever built.

The *Titanic* was huge.

In 1912 the newspapers were full of news
about the *Titanic*.
It was about to make its first voyage.
It was sailing from Southampton in England
to New York in America.

The newspapers stressed
how safe the *Titanic* was.
They said that it could not sink.
In fact, they thought the *Titanic* was unsinkable!

2 Captain Smith

The captain of the *Titanic* was a man
called Captain Smith.
He had about 40 years' experience at sea.

Some years before the *Titanic* set off,
he had told people:

'I have never been in any accident …
of any sort worth speaking about.
I never saw a wreck
and never have been wrecked … .'

June 1911. Captain E J Smith (far right) with other members of the *Olympic*. Captain Smith later became captain of the *Titanic*.

The *Titanic* set sail on 10 April 1912.
Captain Smith wanted to show people
that the *Titanic* could go fast –
even though it was like a big hotel.
He sailed the ship at a speed of 22 knots.

The first few days went smoothly.
The sea was calm and clear.

The Grand Staircase on the *Titanic* used only by the rich and famous.

The *Titanic* was new.

It had all the latest equipment on board.

On April 14 other ships sent the *Titanic* warnings about the ice.

Most of the warnings were ignored.

Only a few were passed on to Captain Smith.

The *Titanic* carried on at a speed of 22 knots.

The wireless room where the warnings about the icebergs were received.

3 Trouble Ahead

One of the crewmen was high on the mast.
His job was to be the lookout.
He could see a large shape
in front of the ship.

It was an iceberg.
It was dead ahead.
It was right in the ship's path.

The lookout struck three bells.
This was the signal that something was dead ahead.
The officer on duty turned the ship.
It made a sharp turn to the right.

At the same time the officer told the crew
to stop the engines.
The huge ship began to turn.
It moved slowly to one side –
but it was too late.
There was a long, grinding sound.
The *Titanic* had scraped the side
of an iceberg.

The passengers were not scared.
The ship had not hit the iceberg.
It was only a scrape.
After all, the *Titanic* was unsinkable.

Some ice fell off the iceberg.
It landed on one of the ship's decks.
The passengers thought that it was fun.
They used bits of ice to put in their drinks.
They carried on with their party.

Second class passengers on board the *Titanic*.

4 Only a Scrape!

Even though there was no party
in the engine room
the crew had no idea what had happened.
They did not know
the iceberg had ripped the side open.
Sea water was pouring in.

The *Titanic* had not hit the iceberg head on.
It might have been better if it had.
There may have been less damage.
At worst the bow of the ship
would have been destroyed.
Maybe the first few sections.

The *Titanic* had turned.
Its side scraped along the iceberg.
The rip in its side was about 100 metres long.
Water was pouring into most sections.

In just ten minutes there was water
over two metres deep in the ship.
The crew tried to pump the water out.
The pumps needed more power.

Power came from boilers heated by fires.
Men worked hard.
They put more and more coal onto the fires.
They tried to get the ship's pumps
working faster.

It was no good.
The water was pouring in too quickly.

The water poured onto the fires.
It flooded the boilers.
The crew had to get out.

Captain Smith knew that it was no good.
It was time to get everybody off the ship.
He sent an SOS message for help.
It would let any nearby ships know
that the *Titanic* needed help.

One ship heard the message.
It was a ship called the *Carpathia*.
It sent a message back.
It told the *Titanic* that it was on its way.

5 Abandon Ship!

Captain Smith gave the order
for passengers to leave the ship.
Women and children were told to go first.
Not very many passengers listened.

They did not believe
that the ship would sink.
After all this was the *Titanic*.
Titanic the unsinkable.

Many women would not go first.
They did not want to leave their husbands.

The first lifeboats left the ship.
Most of them were only half full.
The passengers would not get in them.

After a while the passengers
knew that things were bad.
The *Titanic* was sinking.

They now rushed to get into the lifeboats.
There was not enough room for them all.
They began to panic.

About 1,500 people were still on board
as the last lifeboat was lowered
into the sea.

Captain Smith gave his last radio call
12 minutes later.
He said that the ship was 'lost'.

Some people decided to stay on the ship.
Some jumped overboard into the icy sea.

6 Down She Goes

The huge *Titanic* was sinking.
This giant ship was going down.
The people in the lifeboats watched.
That's all they could do.

They saw the distress flares
lighting up the sky.
They saw the hundreds of passengers
left on board.
They saw husbands, relatives and friends.

They watched as the lights
on the *Titanic* went out.
Then the great ship broke into two.
A few minutes passed and
the *Titanic* sunk into the sea.

It wouldn't be seen again
for another 75 years.

There had been about 2,200 passengers
and crew on board the *Titanic*.
The lifeboats only had room for 1,178.
There were never enough lifeboats
for all the passengers.
Even so, not all of them had been full.
Only about 710 people had used the lifeboats.

Those people who had jumped into
the icy water soon froze to death.

Survivors being rescued by the *Carpathia*. This painting was
drawn from material supplied by a survivor.

7 Rescued

The people in the lifeboats
were freezing cold and in shock.

They waited for about an hour before they saw
the rockets from the *Carpathia*.
This was the ship that had heard
the distress signal.

Another hour passed before the *Carpathia*
rescued the people in the lifeboats.

It was hard to believe that this was all
that was left of the *Titanic*.

For more than 75 years the huge ship
lay hidden under the sea.
Lots of people tried to find it.
In 1986 it was found.

It was more than two-and-a-half miles
under the sea.
The *Titanic* had broken into two pieces.

Pictures were taken of the wreck.
Video film was also taken.
The film shows things scattered around.
There are bottles, cups and saucers
and other things.
There is even the head of a little girl's doll.

The wreck of the *Titanic*
still lies at the bottom of the sea.
Lots of people are still very interested in it.
They want to find out more about it.
They want to be sure about what happened.

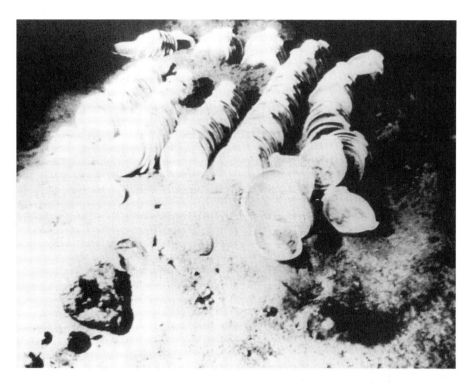

The wreck of the *Titanic* and its possessions still lie at the bottom of the sea.

There have been movies made about the *Titanic*.
There have been lots of stories written about it.

When the *Titanic* sank, about 1,500 people died.
The wreck of the *Titanic* marks their watery grave.

An artist's drawing of the *Titanic*
striking the iceberg.